Boxes c

GW00374076

I can make a ship
out of a box.
I can be a captain.

I can make a rocket
out of a box.
I can be an astronaut.

I can make a plane
out of a box.
I can be a pilot.

I can make a racing car
out of a box.
I can be a driver.

I can make a fire engine
out of a box.
I can be a firefighter.

I can make a train
out of a box.
I can be a train driver.

13

I can make lots of
things out of boxes!

Index